HOW TO DEAL

FEELING GOOD ABOUT YOU

MARIE-THERESE MILLER, Ph.D.

Rourke Educational Media

A Division of Carson Dellosa Education

rourkeeducationalmedia.com

Before Reading: *Building Background Knowledge and Vocabulary*

Building background knowledge can help children process new information and build upon what they already know. Before reading a book, it is important to tap into what children already know about the topic. This will help them develop their vocabulary and increase their reading comprehension.

Questions and Activities to Build Background Knowledge:

1. Look at the front cover of the book and read the title. What do you think this book will be about?
2. What do you already know about this topic?
3. Take a book walk and skim the pages. Look at the table of contents, photographs, captions, and bold words. Did these text features give you any information or predictions about what you will read in this book?

Vocabulary: *Vocabulary Is Key to Reading Comprehension*

Use the following directions to prompt a conversation about each word.

- Read the vocabulary words.
- What comes to mind when you see each word?
- What do you think each word means?

> **Vocabulary Words:**
> - aerobic exercise
> - anxiety
> - endeavors
> - enrich
> - immune system
> - incomparable
> - isolated
> - manageable
> - media
> - meditation
> - persistence
> - self-talk

During Reading: *Reading for Meaning and Understanding*

To achieve deep comprehension of a book, children are encouraged to use close reading strategies. During reading, it is important to have children stop and make connections. These connections result in deeper analysis and understanding of a book.

 Close Reading a Text

During reading, have children stop and talk about the following:

- Any confusing parts
- Any unknown words
- Text to text, text to self, text to world connections
- The main idea in each chapter or heading

Encourage children to use context clues to determine the meaning of any unknown words. These strategies will help children learn to analyze the text more thoroughly as they read.

When you are finished reading this book, turn to page 46 for Text-Dependent Questions and an Extension Activity.

TABLE OF CONTENTS

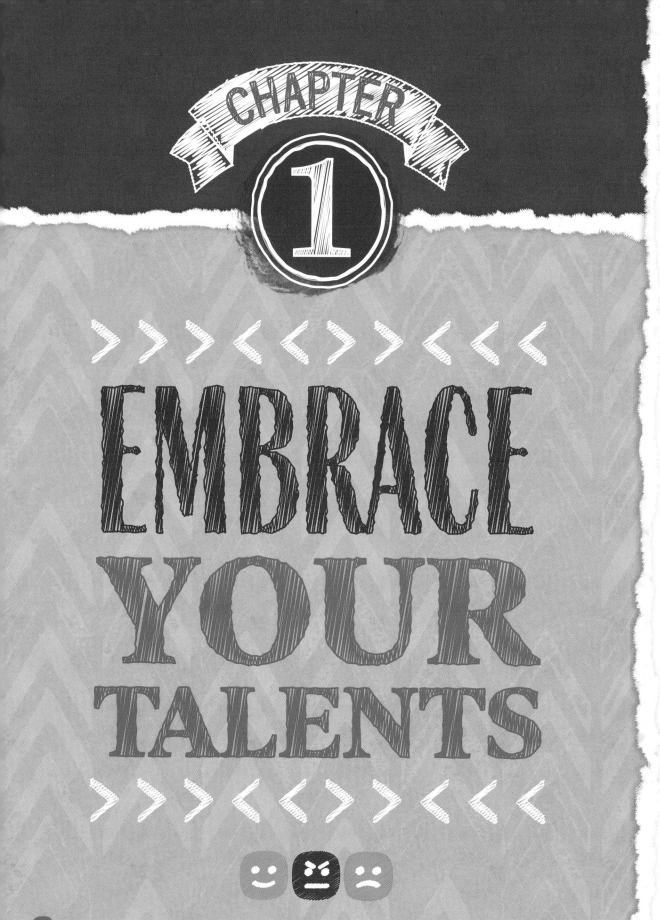

CHAPTER 1

EMBRACE YOUR TALENTS

ily clutched her chest and flopped backward onto her bed. "Your words wound me deeply, Faith," she joked.

Faith rolled her eyes. "You are so dramatic!"

Lily laughed. "I know, right? I really want to be an actress."

"You definitely could," Faith said. "You should audition for the school play."

"I would be too nervous."

"I'll help you practice."

Every day, Faith ran lines with Lily. They even performed a scene for the neighborhood kids.

Finally, Lily landed the role of Mermaid No. 2 in the play—with 12 lines! Faith hugged her. "I knew you could do it."

Self-esteem means how much you value yourself. You have healthy self-esteem if you understand that you possess special talents and so do others. With positive self-esteem, you recognize both your strengths and weaknesses. You feel confident enough to tackle challenges.

Me, Me, Me

Surprisingly, people who brag about themselves actually have low self-esteem. Those with healthy self-esteem feel secure enough about their talents that they don't need to seek approval.

Your self-esteem is under your control. Social worker Lisa Schab writes, "… we can always choose to feel good about ourselves no matter what goes on outside of us." If your sister says you're no rocket scientist, you don't have to accept her opinion. Often, when people say negative things about you, it's a reflection of their problems and not about you.

Reject labels, such as "nerd" or "geek," that people pin on you. You are more than any label suggests. Don't give others limiting labels, either.

Find Cheerleaders

Psychologist Michelle Quilter says, "Surround yourself with people who enhance your self-esteem." You should seek out positive friends—like Faith is to Lily—who will celebrate your fine qualities and encourage your dreams.

To identify your talents, consider what you do well and what interests you. Do you have a clear singing voice or a perfect wrestling takedown? Also, consider your special qualities. Does your offbeat humor keep friends giggling? Maybe your gentle nature has you saving turtles from crawling in the road.

Then, put your talents and qualities into action and sharpen these strengths. Try out for the cross-country team if you are speedy. Practice until you can dodge hanging branches with ease. Are you a lantern fish fan? Then join the marine biology club and learn about more bioluminescent ocean creatures. Improving your skills is sure to raise your self-esteem.

Step outside your comfort zone. Do something different that challenges you–that makes you a bit nervous–just as Lily did with the tryout. Lily took baby steps outside her comfort zone. Every small success gave her the confidence to attempt the next step. And with **persistence** and practice, she might win the starring role next year.

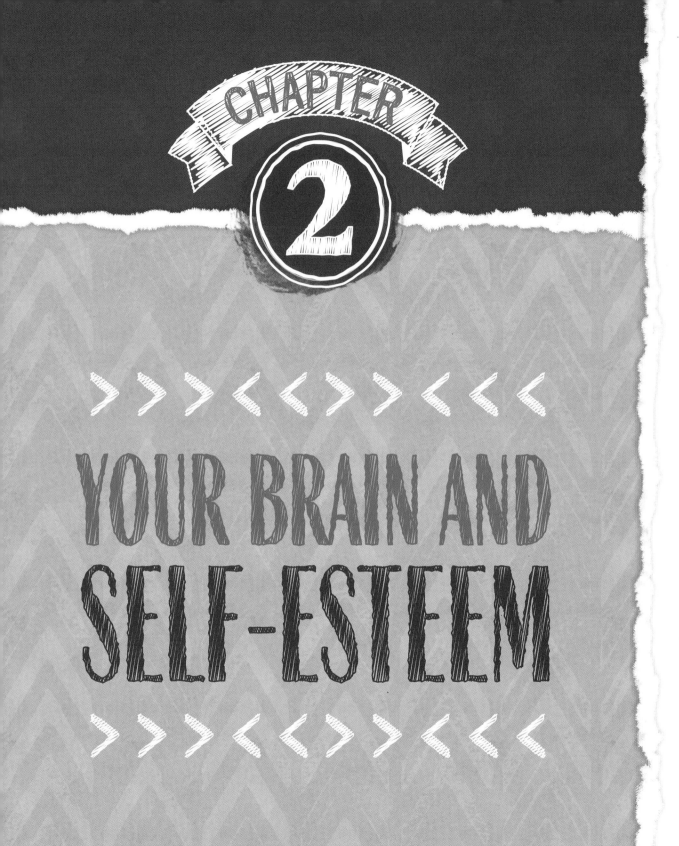

CHAPTER 2

YOUR BRAIN AND SELF-ESTEEM

**O**n his way to lacrosse practice, Ryan tripped over a curb and fell. He sprawled like a starfish on the sidewalk. His whole team saw him go down.

"Are you okay, Ryan?" one of his teammates called.

Ryan jumped up. "I'm fine." His cheeks reddened in embarrassment.

I'm clumsy, he thought. Then, he remembered that his lacrosse coach told him to replace negative thoughts with positive **self-talk**. He tried it:

I was distracted by my deep thoughts.
My muscles sure are flexible.
What a graceful face-plant!

Ryan was smiling by the time he approached his team. "How did you like my sidewalk Superman?"

He laughed, and his teammates laughed with him.

You can improve your self-esteem by changing how you think. Replace negative thoughts about yourself with positive self-talk, as Ryan did after his fall. After Ryan made his thoughts more positive, he felt better about his situation and about himself. In the end—and with a bit of humor—he had everyone laughing.

Kind Thoughts

Educator Meghan Miller says, "We are often our own worst critics." Instead of being tough on yourself, speak to yourself as kindly as you would to a close friend. If a friend failed a test, you wouldn't say, "You are not smart enough." You would probably say, "Go for extra help, and you'll do better."

Optimism and self-esteem go hand in hand. Optimists have a positive attitude about life and about themselves. They believe that things will work out well in the end, so they are more likely to try new things. And success in new **endeavors** builds self-esteem.

Humor breeds optimism. Humor brings joy to everyday life. It makes difficult situations, such as Ryan's fall, more bearable.

Practicing gratefulness also leads to an optimistic attitude. Learn to appreciate the good around you. Take note of raindrops glowing in sunlight. Be thankful for the dandelion that your little brother picked for you. The more you notice good things, the more good things there are to notice.

Mindfulness can keep your attitude positive and reduce **anxiety**. Kathleen Murphy, a mindfulness and **meditation** expert, says, "In mindfulness we come to our senses." When you practice mindfulness, you focus on what your five senses tell you. As you shower, for example, think about how the warm water feels on your skin and how the soap smells. The purpose of mindfulness is to keep your thoughts in the present. Then, you don't dwell on the past or worry about the future.

Kathleen Murphy says that in mindfulness it is important to think about your breathing. Inhale for three counts, exhale for four. This will also trigger your parasympathetic nervous system, which relaxes you. Be grateful for your breathing because it fuels your body.

Brain Changes

Mindfulness meditation actually results in changes in the brain. Using magnetic resonance imaging (MRI), scientists studied people who practiced mindfulness meditation for eight weeks. These people showed a decrease in activity in the brain's amygdala, where the emotion fear is centered.

Mindfulness and mastering a skill often go together. You can be totally absorbed in the present as you learn a Bach prelude on the piano or an ollie on your skateboard. Through mastery, you will build confidence and self-esteem.

Super Sad? There's Help

Sometimes, you might feel alone and think that everyone is against you. You might experience low moods, which can lead to thoughts of self-harm or suicide. Always tell a trusted adult such as a parent, relative, teacher, clergy member, or medical professional who can help you get the support you need. The National Suicide Prevention Lifeline is available 24 hours a day to provide help at 1-800-273-8255.

CHAPTER

3

HEALTHY BODY, HEALTHY SELF-ESTEEM

Chelsea caught her reflection in the locker room mirror. *I'm tiny and strong*, she thought. She hurried into the gym. Today they were doing aerial silks.

Rachel spotted Chelsea at the silks. "Her chicken legs will never be able to climb the silks," Rachel whispered to Gabriel.

Chelsea shinnied up the silks. She wrapped them around herself. She spun, flipped, and did splits.

Rachel's eyes widened. "I wish I could do that."

"I'll teach you," Chelsea told her. "I've been taking lessons for years."

Rachel joined Chelsea at the silks for her first lesson.

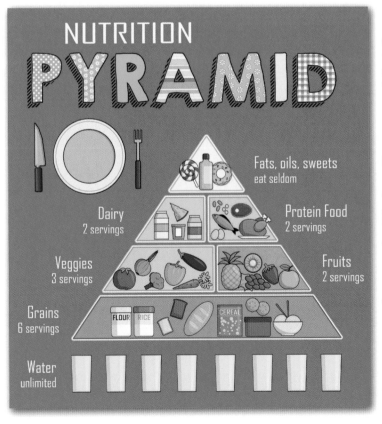

NUTRITION
PYRAMID

Fats, oils, sweets
eat seldom

Dairy
2 servings

Protein Food
2 servings

Veggies
3 servings

Fruits
2 servings

Grains
6 servings

FLOUR RICE

CEREAL

Water
unlimited

When you take good care of your body, you feel better about yourself.

What you eat gives you energy to accomplish your goals. A balanced diet boosts your **immune system** and keeps you healthy. The Mayo Clinic recommends a diet of fruits, vegetables, whole grains, proteins (such as lean meats, eggs, and nuts), and dairy. Many experts suggest skipping soda and sugary drinks in favor of water.

Eating mindfully can be beneficial. Use your five senses while you eat. Savor each bite. This way, you will eat more slowly. You'll give your body a chance to feel full, and you will likely eat less.

Food Choices

Author Michael Pollan says to pick foods with ingredients you can pronounce and with fewer than five ingredients listed. He recommends buying food at the local farmers market, where choices are fresh and nutritious.

Regular exercise keeps your body strong and helps maintain a healthy weight. Exercise reduces feelings of anxiety and depression. With exercise, your body releases endorphins, chemicals that make you feel happier.

The United States government recommends 60 minutes of **aerobic exercise** daily. Three days a week, your routine should also include muscle-strengthening exercises, such as push-ups, and bone-strengthening exercises, such as jumping rope.

The key to sticking with exercise is to pick an activity you love, just as Chelsea chose to do aerial silks. You can find many fun exercise videos online.

You also need to get a solid night's sleep. This will keep you physically well. After a good sleep, you can better focus on schoolwork and succeed. You will also be more cheerful. The CDC (Centers for Disease Control and Prevention) recommends 9 to 12 hours of sleep for children 6 to 12 years old. For 13- to 18-year-olds, 8 to 10 hours are suggested.

To sleep soundly, go to bed at a similar time each night. Have a calming routine, such as taking a warm bath and reading a book. Turn off electronics. They stimulate the brain, and their light disrupts the production of melatonin, the hormone that helps you sleep.

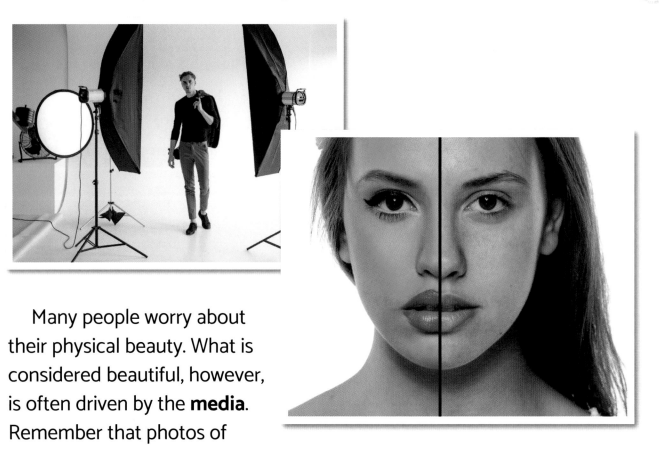

Many people worry about their physical beauty. What is considered beautiful, however, is often driven by the **media**. Remember that photos of models and actors are airbrushed. They also have professional stylists and makeup artists. Real people don't look like that.

Author Claude Clément writes, "Our idea of what looks good changes over time and from place to place." She adds that kindness will always be in style. Chelsea showed her inner beauty when she offered to teach Rachel the silks.

A Weighty Issue

Don't constantly worry about your weight. Dr. Cara Natterson advises, "Ditch the scale at home." Trust your parents and doctor to tell you how you are

Keep It Clean

Grooming is important to your self-esteem. Shower often and brush your teeth. You might pick clothes for comfort or to express your creative style. Either way, be certain your clothes are clean and not wrinkly.

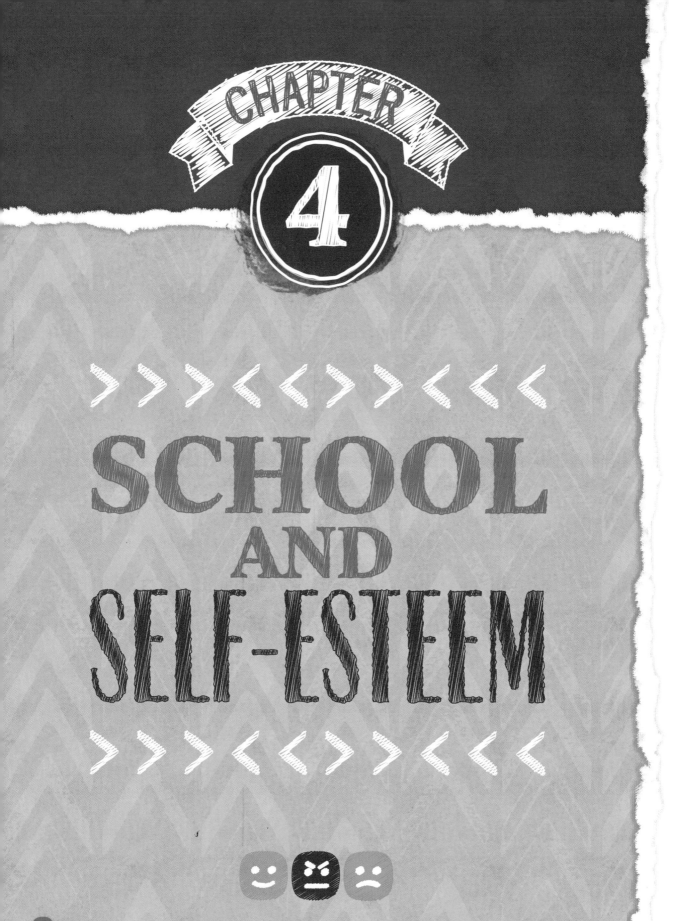

CHAPTER 4

SCHOOL AND SELF-ESTEEM

ngel looked at his graded spelling test and groaned. He thought, *I always spell* friend *the wrong way:* freind.

Angel raised his hand. "Mr. Kenny, I keep misspelling *friend*."

"I have an unusual mnemonic device to help you remember the correct spelling. Do you like to camp?"

Angel nodded. "I really like s'mores melted over a campfire."

"Picture your friend munching his s'more," said Mr. Kenny. "He accidentally backs too close to the campfire and fries his end. He is your 'fri' end."

Angel laughed. "I'll never forget that!"

Your job right now is to go to school and do your best. Working hard at schoolwork will help you succeed and boost your self-esteem.

Jennifer Obrizok, a school psychologist at Millbrook Middle School, says that staying organized and managing time are keys to school success. Use checklists and a calendar to keep track of your assignments.

To do list

1.
2.
3.
4

Break your schoolwork into small parts and tackle them a bit at a time. This makes the work more **manageable** and less overwhelming. You can give yourself little rewards along the way. For example, when you finish reading an assigned chapter in your book, take a short bike ride.

In the classroom, be sure to ask questions, just as Angel did. You are there to learn, and teachers want to teach. When you learn, your self-esteem improves. When teachers teach, their self-esteem gets a boost. Win-win!

Don't be afraid to make a mistake. Everyone does. You can learn from making errors and come back stronger.

Participate in class discussions. Your voice should be heard. Author Susan Cain writes, "Your ideas deserve to be heard and appreciated."

If you are reluctant to speak in class, try these ideas. Sit in the front so you don't notice people looking at you when you talk. Write down what you want to say before you raise your hand. Try adding to somone else's comment. For example, say, "I agree that Victor Frankenstein was selfish, but he surely was a creative thinker."

Assert Yourself

Perhaps you have a concern about a test grade or about completing a project by the due date. Gather your confidence and talk to the teacher. Communication is important to your success in school.

CHAPTER 5

IT FEELS GOOD TO DO GOOD

**E**rin founded a crochet club at school, where the members chatted while they worked with yarn. They even designed original patterns.

One night, Erin's older sister gave birth to twins prematurely. Erin visited the babies in the neonatal intensive care unit (NICU). She noticed them hugging crocheted octopuses. "Those are adorable," Erin said.

The nurse told her, "The tentacles comfort the babies because they are like the umbilical cord. Also, playing with the tentacles keeps the infants from pulling out their wires and tubes."

During crochet club, Erin suggested, "Why don't we make octopuses for preemies?"

The crocheters agreed. When they delivered the handmade toys in person, there were warm hearts and smiles all around.

Volunteering can make you feel good about yourself. If you use your talents in service to others, you make a difference in their lives and give your life added meaning.

Follow your talents and passions when seeking volunteer opportunities, as Erin and her fellow crocheters did. School offers chances to help people, and you don't have to travel. If you love books, volunteer to read to students in the lower grades. Even small acts of kindness can **enrich** your life. Join someone sitting alone in the lunchroom.

Buddy Up

Donna Desimone, a Community Steps to Independence instructor, says many schools have buddy programs that pair you with a student with special needs. These students want more than high fives in the hallway. They crave

Community organizations have places for volunteers as well. Are you a culinary expert? Then prepare meals for the homeless through your church youth group. And don't forget your neighbors. You could dog-sit for the Newfoundland next door.

Volunteering also develops skills, which will improve your self-esteem. Erin and her friends learned new stitches and how to create patterns. By cooking for the homeless, you might learn how to bake chicken tetrazzini for a crowd. You could learn responsibility and dog grooming by caring for your neighbor's pup.

CHAPTER 6

TECHNOLOGY AND SELF-ESTEEM

arrison waved to his grandmother on video chat. "Hi, Nanny."

Nanny smiled broadly. "Hello, pumpkin. Look at that handsome face!"

"What are you up to, Nanny?"

"Organizing pictures from my Mount Hood climb." She shared a photo of herself in cold-weather gear on a snowy mountaintop.

"You are amazing!" Harrison said. "I just got home from Irish step dance class."

"A demonstration, please."

Harrison put on his hard shoes and performed some dance steps—sevens, cuts, and overs—on the kitchen tile.

"Someday, I will be watching you at Carnegie Hall," Nanny told him.

Technology can enhance your self-esteem. However, if you aren't careful, technology can damage how you view yourself.

Technology enriches life. You can use social media and texting to keep in touch with friends and to plan to meet in real life. You can laugh at funny memes and "Aww!" at photos of baby goats. You might video-chat with your loved ones, as Harrison did. They are sure to support and encourage you. Also, reaching out in this way is a kindness on your part, which will make you happy.

However, you need to be cautious with technology. If you spend too much time on your phone or computer, you can become **isolated** and lonely.

Just Walk Away

Psychologist Michelle Quilter advises limiting social media. Viewing a lot of negative news or meanness can make you feel helpless. In your real life, you can make the world a better place.

Scrolling through social media posts, you might see people gorilla trekking in Uganda or having fun at a family reunion surrounded by 100 smiling faces. This could leave you feeling that your life isn't full or that you aren't worthy. Remember that these people only post their best experiences. They aren't putting up photos of the day they had the stomach flu. The posts are all for show. Psychologist Michelle Quilter warns, "Don't compare your insides to other people's outsides."

Truly, you are **incomparable**. You are the only you, and the world is waiting for you to share your special gifts.

ACTIVITY

THE GRATITUDE JAR

Cut construction paper into at least 12 strips. On each strip, use markers or colored pencils to write the name of something you are grateful for. It could be an event, an accomplishment, a person in your life, a pet, a place you love, or a compliment you received. Keep the strips in a jar or other container.

On days when your spirit needs a lift, open the jar and read some of your thoughts of gratitude. They will keep you focused on the positive aspects of your life and give you an optimistic outlook.

GLOSSARY

aerobic exercise (air-OH-bik EK-sur-size): energetic physical activity that strengthens the heart and improves breathing

anxiety (ang-ZYE-i-tee): a feeling of nervousness or fear

endeavors (en-DEV-urz): serious attempts or efforts

enrich (en-RICH): to make something better by adding good things to it

immune system (i-MYOON SIS-tuhm): the body's system, including white blood cells and antibodies, that protects you from disease and infection

incomparable (in-KAHM-pur-ah-buhl): unrivaled, matchless

isolated (EYE-suh-lay-tid): separated from other people

manageable (MAN-aj-ah-bul): capable of being handled with a degree of skill

media (MEE-dee-uh): ways of communicating with large groups of people, such as television, websites, and radio

meditation (med-i-TAY-shuhn): thinking quietly or calmly

persistence (pur-SIS-tens): doing something despite obstacles

self-talk (self-tahk): the act of talking to oneself, either aloud or silently

INDEX

TEXT-DEPENDENT QUESTIONS

1. What is self-esteem?
2. How can you move outside your comfort zone?
3. What is mindfulness and how can it be useful?
4. Which types of exercise do you need to stay healthy?
5. What are some strategies for speaking up in class?

EXTENSION ACTIVITY

Make a list of things you do well and things you enjoy doing. For example, you might be good at mental math or you might enjoy helping young children. Research school or community groups that could use the strengths and qualities you listed. How could you volunteer at these organizations?

BIBLIOGRAPHY

Cain, Susan, Gregory Mone, and Erica Moroz. *Quiet Power: The Secret Strengths of Introverts*. New York: Dial Books for Young Readers, 2016.

Clément, Claude with Melissa Daly. *Don't Be Shy: How to Fit in, Make Friends, and Have Fun—Even If You Weren't Born Outgoing*. New York: Harry N. Abrams, 2005.

Desimone, Donna, TOH. (Program Instructor, Community Steps to Independence, Cresskill, New Jersey), Interview with the author. 27 October 2018.

Gotlink, R. A., R. Meijboom, M. W. Vernooij, et al. "8-Week Mindfulness Based Stress Reduction Induces Brain Changes Similar to Long-Term Meditation Practice-A Systemic Review." *Brain and Cognition*, Vol. 108, March 2016: 32–41.

"How Much Sleep Do I Need?" Centers for Disease Control and Prevention. March 2, 2017. https://www.cdc.gov/sleep/about_sleep/how_much_sleep.html.

Kelly, Nancy, LCSW-R. (Clinical Unit Administrator—Forensics, Dutchess County Department of Community and Behavioral Health, Poughkeepsie, New York), Interview with the author. 22 October 2018.

Miller, Meghan Kathleen, MPH, CHES. (Director of Health Education, The Floating Hospital, Long Island City, New York), Interview with the author. 5 November 2018.

Murphy, Kathleen, MSW, LSW. (Mindful Meditation Specialist, Bluffton, South Carolina). Interview with the author. 19 October 2018.

Natterson, Cara. *The Care and Keeping of You 2: The Body Book For Older Girls*. Middleton, Wisconsin: American Girl Publishing, 2012.

"Nutrition for Kids: Guidelines for a Healthy Diet." Mayo Clinic. https://www.mayoclinic.org/healthy-lifestyle/childrens-health/in-depth/nutrition-for-kids/art-20049335.

Obrizok, Jennifer. (School Psychologist, Millbrook Middle School, Millbrook, New York), Interview with the author. 12 October 2018.

Pollan, Michael. *In Defense of Food: An Eater's Manifesto*. New York: The Penguin Press, 2008.

Quilter, Michelle, PsyD., CASAC, DBT-LBC. (Director of Dialectical Behavior Therapy Program, Lifeskills South Florida, Deerfield Beach, Florida), Interview with the author. 5 November 2018.

Schab, Lisa M., LCSW. *Self Esteem for Teens: Six Principles for Creating the Life You Want*. Oakland, California: Instant Help Books, 2016.

U.S. Department of Health and Human Services. "Physical Activity Guidelines for Americans: Youth Physical Activity Recommendations." https://health.gov/paguidelines/2008/midcourse/youth-fact-sheet.pdf.

ABOUT THE AUTHOR

Marie-Therese Miller is the author of the *Dog Tales* series about working dogs, *Managing Responsibilities*, and *Rachel Carson*. She holds a Ph.D. in English from St. John's University, where her scholarly focus was James Thurber and humor. Miller counts her husband, John, and their five children among her closest friends.

www.rourkeeducationalmedia.com

PHOTO CREDITS: Cover Photos (Top) © Daisy Daisy, (Bottom) © Monkey Business Images; Page 4-5: istock.com | kali9; Page 6-7: istock.com | AaronAmat, Shutterstock.com | Monkey Business Images, istock.com | izkes; Page 8-9: Shutterstock | Monkey Business Images, istock.com | Bronwyn8, istock.com | monkeybusinessimages; Page 10-11: istock.com LivingImages; Page 12-13: istock.com | Daisy-Daisy, istock.com | monkeybusinessimages, istock.com | Daisy-Daisy, Page 14-15: istock.com | torwai, istock.com | shironosov, istock.com AntonioGuillem; Page 16-17: istock.com | Thon_Varirit, istock.com | orodenkoff, shutterstock.com | SeventyFour; Page 18-19: istock.com | master1305; Page 20-21: istock.com | Lisovskaya, istock.com | MedejaJa, istock.com | RossHelen; Page 22-23: shutterstock.com | Denis Kuvaev, istock.com | Ben_Gingell, istock.com | Motortion; Page 24-25: istock.com | igor_kell, istock.com | VladimirFLoyd, istock.com | marieclaudelemay; Page 26-27: istock.com | Wavebreakmedia; Page 28-29: istock.com | lisafx, istock.com | arsenisspyros, istock.com | Deagreez; Page 30-31: istock.com | monkeybusinessimages, istock.com | JackF; Page 32-33: istock.com | Vitalij Sova, shutterstock.com | de2marco; Page 34-35: istock.com | Daisy-Daisy, istock.com | lisafx; Page 36-37: shutterstock.com | New Africa, istock.com | McIninch; Page 38-39: istock.com | 2p2play; Page 40-41: istock.com | monkeybusinessimages, istock.com | SeventyFour, istock.com | DGLimages; Page 42-43: istock.com | jacoblund, istock.com | marieclaudelemay, istock.com | marieclaudelemay; Page 44-45: istock.com | nastenkapeka

Edited by: Kim Thompson

Produced by Blue Door Education for Rourke Educational Media. Cover and interior design by: Jennifer Dydyk

Library of Congress PCN Data

Feeling Good About You / Marie-Therese Miller, Ph.D.
(How to Deal)
ISBN 978-1-73161-486-5 (hard cover)
ISBN 978-1-73161-293-9 (soft cover)
ISBN 978-1-73161-591-6 (e-Book)
ISBN 978-1-73161-696-8 (e-Pub)
Library of Congress Control Number: 2019932377

Rourke Educational Media
Printed in the United States of America,
North Mankato, Minnesota